THE PHYSICIAN'S GUIDE TO FINANCIAL FREEDOM: GETTING STARTED AS A CONSULTANT

How to Successfully Launch and Brand Your Unique Skill Sets to Position, Leverage, and Capitalize on Niche Consulting Opportunities

CHRISTOPHER H. LOO, MD-PhD

Paperback *ISBN:* 978-1-0801-85047-

Hardback ISBN: ISBN: 9798428083781

Disclaimer: This is my own personal story building my consulting business. I am here to inform and educate the reader, and give them experience-based wisdom. I am not advocating any financial services, products, or investment plans. For tax-related or legal matters, please consult a tax accountant, attorney, or advisor.

There are sections of the book that include strong language. I have added this not to offend anyone, but in order to achieve a polarizing effect and to strongly emphasize my beliefs against the status quo and mainstream group-think. If this truly does offend you, please either skip ahead, put the book down altogether, or reach out and engage with me.

This book is dedicated to God, to my parents (Sue Hwa and Lian-Sim Loo), to my wife, Annie Phu, my brother, Nathaniel H. Loo, MD, my nieces (Tiffany, Tina, Sophia, Aubrey, Olivia, Sabrina), and to my nephew, Kai.

Books by Christopher H. Loo

How I Quit My Lucrative Medical Career and Achieved Financial Freedom Using Real Estate (You Can, Too!)

The Physician's Guide to Financial Freedom Using Stocks and Options

The Physician's Guide to Financial Freedom: Getting Started as a Consultant

The Physician's Guide to Financial Freedom: Becoming a Freelance Writer

CONTENTS

CHRISTOPHER LOO

PREFACE

IT IS 1:47 A.M. on the East Coast, in late July 2019. I am finishing the edits on my third book. Two years ago, my plan was to write one book a year. I have completed three books during that time frame and plan on finishing my fourth book by the end of this year, making it a total of *two* books per year.

As I watch this book unfold, I am simply amazed. I struggled with my first book and with getting my ideas onto paper in a clear, concise, and effective manner (to the vexation of my editor, Kathryn!). It was long, wordy, disorganized, and had no point to it.

But after many stressful months, I managed to finish it in a nine-month timeframe. I promoted it at several conferences where I was speaking and was surprised that it sold so well. It became profitable in less than two months and had five-star reviews.

My second book was easier to write and edit, and it was released within six months. I sold twice as many copies of my second book as I did my first in the same amount of time.

Now, I am really happy with my third book. I am confident that this book has a bright future.

My ideas took shape and came to paper much faster. My message was clearer and more effective, and it has come together all in the span of less than three months. As I think back, my past and future books will be used as a platform to transform, inspire, educate, spread, and sell my message.

At this current point in time, I have four other book ideas (possibly more) that I'm contemplating completing and getting out there in the next few years.

A book is a creative work. It takes form from a rough idea and then is developed and polished in a way that has the power to transform, elevate, and change people's reality. A book is worth the hard work and creative stresses because it can touch and reach people. It takes the reader into another world, one with cutting-edge, innovative ideas, and fascinating characters and stories.

I fell in love with books when I was eleven years old because it was one of the only ways to escape my childhood reality. I loved reading about psychology, persuasion, personal development, and business. I currently love science fiction, because it gives me a glimpse into what the future can hold, much like it did when I watched *The Jetsons* as an eight-year-old. It is a glimpse into another reality, a moment in time; a view into the author's headspace about his or her thoughts, ideas, and feelings.

If there's any book of mine that I would personally recommend (without any profit motive), it would be this book. I'm glad you've picked it up to read. It contains most if not all of my ideas in my first and second books, but in a more refined and potent form.

I am grateful that you've invested your hard-earned time, money, and energy in this book. I am happy to share my thoughts, experience, and time with you. Much like a movie, please sit back, relax, enjoy, and get ready to be informed, entertained, educated, and inspired.

CHAPTER 1

INTRODUCTION

THIS IS THE THIRD book in my *Physician's Guide to Financial Freedom* series. My first book, *How I Quit My Lucrative Medical Career and Achieved Financial Freedom,* describes my personal story of going from frustrated physician battling the status quo to my becoming financially free using real estate. The second book, *The Physician's Guide to Financial Freedom Using Stocks and Options,* details how to strategically use stocks and options in your financial portfolio for additional income, financial freedom, and wealth generation/ preservation.

Now, I've turned my consulting experience into my third book, and writing it has been one of the most fulfilling experiences of my career. Why? Because consulting is one field where you can forge your own path. You can create your own experiences. You are in control of your own destiny. And it is extremely lucrative.

I love writing, speaking, coaching, and consulting. I am an avid fan of using technology to battle the status quo.

In the consulting field, you have so many opportunities to market, sell, and create your own personal brand in the professional world. You get to be a creator. You get to be innovative.

You also get to charge what you're worth. You are paid based on what the marketplace is willing to pay. There are no insurance hassles, and no need to play up to the CEO, some department head, supervisor, or middle manager.

You can have no boss, if you choose. You can set your own hours. You can set your own schedule. You can choose or decline any given projects or clients. You get to say "No," sometimes for the first time in your life!

Unlike real estate and stocks, which are tangible assets that generate different forms of income, consulting is a separate source of income that involves you promoting, marketing, and selling yourself, your skills, and your services (all of which are intangible assets) to your specific market niche. You, yourself, become the asset.

You brand yourself as an expert, who can teach and guide others, create experiences and share your knowledge. This is the ultimate form of service, one where you get to contribute your unique gifts to the world.

As a consultant, you also have the ability to create unique products, which you can then market, promote, and sell. I like to refer to these products as "extensions" of yourself. This adds additional leverage, because these products become assets, which in turn lead to additional streams of passive income. In addition, these products can be stepping stones from which to launch future products that can address or solve particular niche needs.

Here are some of the **key benefits** of a consulting career:

1. No "boss"
2. Not being tied to any particular employer
3. You can walk away at any time
4. Ability to say "no" to any particular assignment or engagement
5. Variety
6. Novelty
7. Setting your own hours
8. Option to work remotely
9. Setting your own rates
10. Creative
11. Rewarding
12. Carve your own path
13. Opportunities to travel
14. Tax advantages

15. Expenses (hotel, food, transportation, education, miscellaneous) are either covered by the client or deductible as consulting business expenses

In my experience, there are also a few disadvantages to the consulting career choice, including:

1. Startup environment
2. Variable income
3. Variable schedule
4. Instability
5. Challenges to getting clients
6. Challenges to getting paid
7. Challenges to getting repeat clients
8. Need to continuously produce
9. Travel
10. Meetings

The key here is, if you are starting out in your own niche, you will have to carve your own path. It is less likely that you'll land a highly lucrative consulting assignment right off the bat. You will need to start small (much like starting your medical practice), build your client base, gain experience and promote yourself, as you figure out ways to provide more and more value to your clients and become consistently more valuable to them, as you work together.

Your progress to a successful consulting career will be enhanced by attaining a deeper knowledge of technology (notably, social media skills), as well as developing your marketing and promotion efforts, through writing books, blogging, networking, and doing speaking engagements. But practice in these areas will not only improve your skill sets in marketing, promoting, advertising, and branding yourself as an authority, but they will also lead to future products, assignments, speaking engagements, and consulting assignments. The process repeats and compounds upon itself.

Additionally, with recent technological advances, the barriers to entry for this career have been lowered, thereby providing less friction for adopting new consulting business ideas.

One misconception is that people transitioning into consulting think it will be much easier than their previous occupations. This career will indeed offer more freedom and flexibility, but it will also be a lot of hard work. In addition, a consulting career can often involve a lot of traveling and staying in different hotels, which means time away from family, time spent at airports, endless phone calls, and constant client meetings. You will need to put in a lot of hours, investing your time, energy, and money.

One piece of advice I give my private coaching clients: You do not want to leave your current job in order to "own" another job. A lot of individuals quit their jobs to "go out on their own," but then realize, instead of their job owning them, they now own another job. If you're looking to work "on" your business instead of "in" your business, I recommend, as Robert Kiyosaki says, "moving from the employed, self-employed quadrants into the business owner or investor quadrants." But those are different skill sets and topics I've written about in my first book, plus I will touch upon them in future books.

The bottom line is that in consulting, there will be a different type of work, but you will still have to "work hard." Those of you who are interested in more lifestyle-freedom businesses or work-life balance, I recommend you explore other career avenues in addition to consulting, but each has its own set of issues and specific challenges.

If you decide to dive in, despite these caveats, I am certain that you will be rewarded with time and flexibility, creativity and happiness, despite the fact that your consulting work will invariably involve a lot of travel, meetings, phone calls, reports, communicating, and negotiating.

Also, as you start your own consulting business, you will be in the self-employed category. While you will still be trading your time for money, you will now be in charge, rather than answering to an employer, a hospital, an institution, boss, or middle manager. This control and independence are what give you the freedom and flexibility to allocate your time and efforts as you see fit. The work and hours you put in will be for *you*, in this scenario, rather than for someone else.

Another correlate to being self-employed is, depending upon how you structure your business, self-employed entrepreneurs (solo-preneurs) may pay higher income taxes, because of the extra 7.5% tax contributions to Social Security, Medicare, and Medicaid previously paid by your employer. Thus, when you are out on your own, you will have a variable income, in addition to being required to cover both employer and employee shares of tax contributions toward Social Security, Medicare, and Medicaid. This is a key reason why the majority of individuals do not want to leave their job and instead prefer the stability of being an employee. However, for everything there is a hidden cost. For the price of succumbing to fear and failing to take calculated risks, one is forgoing personal growth and missed opportunities, and possibly failing to reach their full potential.

However, as you achieve more success, grow your consulting business, and become a business owner, your taxes will decrease substantially due to the number of favorable tax savings opportunities. Again, I am not a tax attorney or tax advisor, so please get professional advice on these types of matters.

Not only does a business owner have more advantages in terms of taxes, he or she has more leverage in terms of using other people's resources (time, money, talents, possessions, assets) as well as the ability to serve more and more people on a more significant level.

CHAPTER 2:

MY STORY

AS I EXPLORED IN my first two books, I first pursued a career in medicine, thinking it would make me "happy," make my wife, family, and community see me as a "success," and bring me fulfillment.

If you're intrigued, I invite you to read on. But for those of you who have read my first two books or who aren't as interested in how I came to making the consulting-career decision, feel free to skip ahead to Chapter 3.

When I eventually reached my goal of getting into an orthopedic surgery residency, in 2007, I found myself wondering quite a few things:

> ➤ "Do I really want to do this for the rest of my life?"
> ➤ "After all of that hard work to get here, this is not what I expected—why?"
> ➤ "Is this *it*?"
> ➤ "Why do I feel like I'm being handcuffed in all different directions—by taxes, mortgage, hospital mandates, insurance mandates, avoiding litigation, debt, and societal obligations—while folks in Washington, D.C., on Wall Street, and the already rich are getting ahead faster and faster, in terms of time, success, freedom, and financial status?"

Looking back, I realized my real passion lay in seeking out new markets and opportunities, niches and trends, especially in technology. I was really intrigued by building businesses and developing additional revenue streams around these emerging societal trends. I was interested in more of a creative career but felt stifled as a physician, doing the same things over and over for less and less with more and more hassles.

I was also interested in the entrepreneurial spirit—reading, traveling, learning, along with the ability to develop something that had the potential to change the way we lived. I loved the idea of having no boss, of not being tied to any job, and of working only with people who shared my vision and passions. I liked how you could live and work anywhere you wanted, anytime you wanted, while creating and contributing my unique gifts to society on a more significant level.

Entrepreneurship also resonated with my being fed up with the status quo, the shitty educational system, the dysfunctional health care system, political and business corruption, the destruction of the environment, corporate greed, and white-collar crime. I was sick of being a corporate cog, and seeing the rich get richer and richer, while the poor and middle class struggled, falling further and further behind.

I had observed how the transformative power the Information Age had super-charged development of the Internet (Google, Yahoo, eBay, Facebook, Netflix, Amazon), smartphones, social media (Facebook, Instagram, YouTube, Snapchat), and sharing services (Uber, Lyft, Airbnb), making our world more efficient and effective. And it is on track to inspire even more transformation, through innovative technologies developed in China, artificial intelligence, virtual, augmented reality, 3D printing, autonomous vehicles, and machine learning.

My passion and interests showed me that I didn't have to work for anybody or anyone, if I didn't want to. My real motivation in life was to be financially independent and free, not dependent upon the economy, any job or market, any upturn or downturn. I was ideally suited to be my own boss, so I could buy what I needed, travel, and do anything I wanted.

So, for the last twelve years, I have been a successful entrepreneur and investor. I have traveled the world writing books, and speaking to audiences about the importance of financial education, entrepreneurship, and financial freedom.

In the meantime, I have developed my consulting career into a six-figure business. I am involved in hospital-based electronic health record implementation, telemedicine, executive coaching, writing, and speaking. My consulting career has been the busiest, most intense period of my life, while also being the most rewarding financially as well as in terms of personal growth, experience, and learning.

That is why I'm now writing this book for you, to share my knowledge with you.

One of the most common phrases I hear from my beginning coaching clients is, "I am not worthy, because I am not a practicing physician."

My response? This is total BS! Plus, it makes absolutely no sense. This is a socially conditioned belief, whereby society and the medical community "think," if you are not actively practicing, "something" had to have happened. Sued. Fired. Deficient. Mental illness. *Whatever*.

Life is full of ups and downs and unexpected surprises, filled with twists and turns, adventures and heartbreaks, setbacks and failures. If life was a straight path, full only of successes, we would not grow, as humans. And in that case, we also would likely not be challenging ourselves to the fullest extent.

I think about some of my colleagues who have seen their families torn apart due to divorce. Are they lesser than, because of this? I don't think so.

The same applies to doctors not currently practicing medicine.

I am extremely skeptical about the fact that you've never failed at something that really mattered to you.

The bottom line is this: No one is responsible for your happiness except for yourself. Why would you let people who barely know you dictate how you think, perceive, feel, or respond? Why would you even care what they think or want? It took me a long time to internalize this belief, myself.

Think about this: most lawyers use their degrees *outside* of actively practicing law (in investment banking, finance, politics, or business). Are they shunned by their colleagues and society, because they don't go to work in a courtroom every day?

I highly doubt it.

And a number of these trained lawyers work in Washington D.C. and create a lot of the rules and regulations that benefit them and their constituents! Talk about "A" students working for "C" students. As a sophomore in college, I attended an inspiring talk by Dr. James "Red" Duke, the famous University of Texas trauma surgeon, who said that Washington, D.C., lawyers, Wall Street, insurance, and Big Pharma have a license to legally steal from the masses.

Or what about an MBA holder? There are tons of MBAs who are doing non-corporate work, becoming entrepreneurs, working at startups, or doing consulting.

What about those with PhDs? There are a ton of PhDs who are starting their own companies, getting into consulting, or becoming entrepreneurs rather than pursuing the traditional academic route.

The list goes on and on, the only point being the same should apply for anyone with an MD. Just because you don't go to work every day in a hospital doesn't mean you are lesser than anyone else. As such, you shouldn't be looked down upon.

In fact, my opinion is it's a waste of time, potential, and resources to spend ten to fifteen years of your life, getting into over $500,000 in student loan debt (that could buy a nice-sized house or even more!), killing yourself staying up late, while your friends and colleagues are building their careers ten years ahead of you, are out socializing and building their families, while you are immersing yourself in a competitive, scarcity-based herd/crowd mentality *JUST* to get into medical school.

Then, going through four-plus years of medical school plus four to eight years of postgraduate training, all the while being treated and paid like "shit," married to your student loans, mortgage, and job, in order to finally be stuck in a hospital, working twelve-plus hours per day, while you are feeling miserable, constantly listening to the same complaints over and over, doing the same procedures over and over, worrying if you're going to get sued, filling out excessive administrative paperwork, going through excessive insurance hurdles to get paid, and answering to people who have half as much education, experience, and training as you—just to make an annual income of $300,000 or more.

That is not worth it! You can make that amount of income in less amount of time and with less suffering, all while having a better quality of life, being happier and healthier, spending time with friends and family, growing and learning, paying less in taxes, and not being married to your job, mortgage, and student loans.

Why start ten to fifteen years behind, over half a million dollars in debt, and being a "slave"? You are losing out due to the opportunity cost in terms of time, debt, energy, and investment involved.

This used to be sound strategy, because your income as a physician would make up for all of that lost time. Not anymore. Due to inflation, taxes, debt, and managed care, you are absolutely losing out—starting out behind, deeply in debt, and now dependent upon an employer for your income. Why have your overall quality of life suffer?

If that is the life you envision, then great. But that is not my dream. I do not want to be a corporate "cog." No, thank you.

This is not an effective way of scaling your efforts and time, because time and energy are finite resources. With patient care, you can only see one patient, one case at a time. It is tedious, cumbersome, and time-consuming. There is simply no scale in it, and it will burn you out. Again, all remnants from the Industrial Age, where we hoarded resources and participated in scarcity-based group-think.

Instead, you want to separate yourself from your time in a way that allows you to scale or leverage your time more effectively (through increasing your per-hour rate, hiring multiple staff, employing multiple income opportunities, or establishing passive income streams).

The most successful and wealthy physicians achieved their wealth not through patient care, but through other means—inventions, consulting, speaking, writing, or becoming entrepreneurs. Think about Dr. Wayne Dyer, Dr. Deepak Chopra, or Dr. Sanjay Gupta.

Now that I've gotten off my rant, let's move on to subsequent chapters which are all about building, growing, leveraging, and protecting your brand. And how to spot, create, and capitalize on niche opportunities instead of just working for your money.

CHAPTER 3

YOUR CONSULTING NICHE

JUST AS IN ANY FIELD, you need to specialize and become an expert in something. You need to have a broad, strong base of fundamental knowledge and a skill set. But what will differentiate you from the rest of the pack is how you narrow your focus.

In the consulting field, what are the particular areas in which you have specific expertise that no one else does? This is your unique experience. What is it that you can be the only and best in the world at? This is your USP—unique selling proposition. This is your competitive advantage.

Identify this, and focus all of your efforts and energy, and you become indispensable, irreplaceable, and unstoppable. This is what Steve Jobs, Bill Gates, Mark Zuckerberg, Michael Jordan, Tiger Woods have done, and the list goes on. These are the individuals who have changed the world by keying in on this one principle.

If you identify this, you are more than halfway there, my friend. After that, it is all about strategically executing and leveraging your time and efforts.

You want to be a big fish in a small pond.

You want to build a "moat" around your brand, your skillset, and your industry.

Those who invent niches will have the greatest potential and most opportunities. This not only will set you apart from the rest of the pack, but, rather than being a "jack of all trades, master of none," you can establish yourself as the master of one particular trade and build multiple streams of passive income around that.

Think about economic leaders and success stories: Apple, Facebook, Google, Airbnb, Uber, Lyft.

You want to be a trendsetter.

You want to be creating niches.

You want the masses to be following you.

You don't want to be following the masses.

You want to avoid crowd- and herd-based group thinking.

Paris and Milan do this in the fashion world: they set the fashion trends every season, and the fashion world eats it up.

The most successful individuals have differentiated themselves by specifically honing in on and refining their particular craft and skillset, and by becoming the best at what they are good at.

What one particular skill or area can you be so good at as to differentiate yourself from others? This is what you need to identify, in order to take your first steps at financial freedom when entering the consulting field.

Let me give you a few examples of the consulting niches I have developed and worked in:

- ➢ Electronic health records implementation
- ➢ TeleMedicine
- ➢ Health care startup optimizing tablet-based app for optimal medical billing and coding
- ➢ Executive coaching for high net worth clients
- ➢ Being a keynote speaker
- ➢ Writing books based on the niche businesses I've created, in order to create passive income streams from my unique skillsets and life experiences

The best way to determine your consulting niche

I recognize it takes a great deal of introspection and thought, to identify and qualify your own consulting niche or niches.

My recommendation is that you start by identifying your top three strengths, skillsets, or experiences.

What are your top three fields of interest or expertise?

For me, I am good at speaking, writing, promoting, marketing, branding, advertising, and selling. I love technology and identifying current and upcoming trends. My unique selling proposition, the one experience that nobody had, was that I was fed up with the inefficient, bureaucratic medical profession, and I retired from the field at a time when everybody thought I was crazy. Ten years later, though, it was clearly the best decision for me. And now, those who thought I'd never make it are coming to me for words of wisdom, advice, encouragement, and guidance. For a long time, I thought I was the only person to leave behind a lucrative medical career. When I found out there was a massive and growing segment of burned-out physicians, I used that experience to reach out to other physicians.

There is no substitute for experience, because that is someone's unique, individual story.

So, before going on to the next chapter, spend ten minutes brainstorming potential consulting niches that may be of interest to you, based on what we talked about in this chapter.

The top five skillsets needed to be successful at consulting

1. Negotiating and setting boundaries: having the ability to walk away and/or to say no. A mentor once told me, in order to truly be successful, you have to be unapologetically polarizing. This means being authentically you. If you define this boundary, certain marketing segments will 100% love you, and a portion will hate on you. You will know, when this occurs, you are on the right path. While your goal is to tap into a particular market segment and create a loyal following, if you were to choose between having haters versus being ignored, I would choose the first option (see section on haters in Chapter 10).

2. Networking: this is a crucial skillset. You never know when a particular contact will

lead to your next assignment, your next deal, or your next client.

Effective networking takes practice. A study conducted showed that those who go out and socialize with the intent to develop friendships and professional contacts are much more likely to be successful than someone who makes straight A's but does not socialize. I made this mistake early on, thinking that getting into medical school was just about getting stellar grades, while my classmates and colleagues did just as well or better, while having better social lives.

Your professional network is your net worth. A fundamental fact is that your business, your career, is all about people. We are in the people business, which is about trust, integrity, communication, boundaries, value, status, emotional connection, likeability, and friendliness. There are a number of ways to be successful on the networking front, which will be the subject of one of my next books!

3. Marketing, selling, advertising, and branding your products and services.

4. The ability to convey value, status, and boundaries in a professional, firm, yet friendly and positive way. The best speakers, coaches, consultants, managers, and leaders have this ability to convey their message and get their points across effectively, efficiently, and in a collaborative way. This, along with networking, is a key skillset for becoming a successful consultant.

5. Ability to brand, market, advertise, and sell yourself, both in person and online. More on this in Chapter 4.

CHAPTER 4

BUILDING YOUR CONSULTING BRAND

IN TODAY'S DAY AND AGE, your brand is the key to future-proofing your consulting business. The more you can distinguish yourself from the rest of the pack, the better off you're going to be.

Most people think that being everything to everyone will be the key to their success. Not only will this strategy diffuse your efforts and dissipate your influence, it will lead to being distracted, scattered, and a people-pleaser in all of the wrong ways.

Much like you do as a unique individual, in a business you want to specialize. The goal is to be so great within a specific niche that you're the only one who does what you do or who people think of when they want or need help in that niche. In so doing, you will be able to create, redefine, and shape trends and industries. You become a trendsetter rather than following the herd.

You do not want to be average.

You do not want to be better than your competition. Think about the last sentence. I know it doesn't make sense, but you want to be *so* different and great at your niche that you're the first and only one in it. Your ambition is to make the idea of competition nonexistent.

This will future-proof your business against competitors, changes in the economy, or other potential disruptive forces.

The idea is that you don't compete (this is based on a scarcity and hoarding mentality), but instead create from your own set of strengths and skillsets. Some examples of this concept include:

* Warren Buffett—who recommended that the surest way of not becoming obsolete is to "build a moat around your brand."
* Nike
* Starbucks
* Coke
* McDonalds
* Tiffany's
* Facebook
* Google
* Netflix
* Apple
* Gucci
* Prada
* Tony Robbins
* Donald Trump
* Robert Kiyosaki
* Marc Cuban
* Gary Vaynerchuck
* Michael Jordan
* Tiger Woods
* Dennis Rodman
* Kim Kardashian

* Madonna
* Lady Gaga
* Pink

Again, this list could go on. Most of the population has interacted with one of these (in)famous brands at one point or another in their lifetime.

I do not see any doctors here. And when you look up world's wealthiest doctors, many of them are non-practicing; they have become investors or entrepreneurs, started businesses, and monetized their inventions.

Out of all the examples above, the newest generation of influencers has learned how to promote, market, and brand themselves skillfully, using social media to reach their target audience. Branding yourself is one of the top-five key skillsets that will define your success as a consultant. Not only will it put you in position to leverage and scale your consulting business, it will protect you while also promoting you.

Also, not only do you need to have the skill of building, developing, and protecting your brand, you must develop the ability to position and leverage your brand in order to capitalize on niche consulting opportunities for success in today's marketplace.

Branding involves people's perceptions of you, your skillset, and your experience, how you market and advertise, plus the products and services you create and/or the unique experiences you provide for your clients, so they become repeat customers and refer you to their friends, colleagues, and family. Ideal branding turns clients into raving fans.

In the book, *WikiBrands*, the concept of a brand has evolved from something that corporations would dictate to the consumer through traditional media (TV, radio, newspaper) in the Industrial Age, into an interactive-based relationship between brands and customers relying on social media channels. In effect, customers are able to have more choice and options in the marketplace based on what they need, want, prefer, and identify with, rather than what has been conventionally available.

Think of a brand as everything that you stand for. Your values, your message, your company, your trust, your reputation, your integrity, all of your systems, operations, infrastructure, employees, the customer experience, customer relationships, your marketing messages, your content, your productions, and your intellectual property.

That being said, let's look at what are the different levels and effectiveness of branding. How do you go about this?

Beginning level (hundred to thousands of followers):

- ✓ Ability to create and promote. This is a matter of developing a strategy, coming up with a game plan, sticking to the schedule, and executing.
- ✓ Ability to create great, unique content through photos, videos, articles, blog posts
- ✓ Ability to take that content and leverage it onto social media

Intermediate level (tens-of thousands-plus followers):

- ✓ Ability to attract user engagement
- ✓ Ability to get followers
- ✓ Ability to get comments
- ✓ Ability to get likes
- ✓ Ability to get subscribers
- ✓ Ability to get people to purchase your products and services

Advanced levels (hundred thousand to millions of followers):

- ✓ People to sign up for your blogs, vlogs, social media, YouTube, Facebook, Instagram, Twitter
- ✓ Ability to get multiple people to buy your products and services through content generation and user participation
- ✓ People to give you great reviews, feedback
- ✓ People talk about/refer you to their friends, family, colleagues, and co-workers
- ✓ Ability to attract a following
- ✓ Ability to create tribes

- ✓ Ability to attract people who become lifelong fans
- ✓ Becoming an influencer

Branding in the digital economy

Before the industrial revolution, most economies were based on the markets—buyers and sellers. Once everything became industrialized, where goods and services were manufactured, production and distribution became standardized, and organizations arose that led to corporations, management, hierarchy, and bureaucracy.

With the digital age, the buying and selling of goods and services has evolved from markets and organizations onto platforms. These platforms have allowed greater and easier access to products and services that are increasingly more complex and of higher value. The existing technology has shifted from human capital and resources to technological capital and resources, while key investments are made into logistics, supply chain, and infrastructure.

So, in this age, which has evolved from bartering goods and services (Craigslist) to buying and selling (eBay, Amazon, Facebook) to renting out homes and cars, (Airbnb, Uber, Lyft), the platforms have developed the ability to digitize and scale trust. Today, strangers are allowed to rent parts of others' homes without the owner's being there, or they feel comfortable getting into a car with someone they hardly know.

How does this relate to branding? You must, as a consultant, be able to brand in the digital age on any and all digital platforms, both current and upcoming.

Branding is another medium of trust. If you were in a different city, would you buy coffee from a random mom-and-pop shop? Or at the local Starbucks? The stronger your brand name is, the stronger your following.

Another thing to note is that your brand is built up over time. It does not occur overnight. Much like trust is scaled over Ebay, Amazon, AirBNB, Uber, and Lyft, through user reviews and user ratings, your brand reputation is built up over time.

CHAPTER 5

PROTECTING AND ENHANCING YOUR BRAND

THERE ARE NUMEROUS CAUTIONARY tales of companies being wiped out in an instant because they didn't understand how to protect their brand. For example, consider Napster, the former online music sharing site. It had all of its music files in a central location, so, when artists and record labels went to sue the startup, it was gone almost as fast as it had arisen. Napster had one single point of failure.

In contrast, look at the file-sharing site BitTorrent. It is a decentralized platform, where users go to get bits and pieces of digital data they seek (music, videos, files). It is less risky than

Napster, because the "risk" is distributed over the entire network versus being centrally located in one point in time and space. Since everything is moving to online streaming now, this is less of an issue than before, but you get the point. Still, people have been pirating paid streaming movies and videos and then posting them on free online streaming sites.

I am not condoning pirating or copyright violations here. I am showing you an example of how, due to extremely fast market trends, you can either be ahead of or behind the curve. And with distributed risk versus centralized risk, how you can forecast any potential attacks to your business brand. You want to have multiple avenues and channels, in the event your reputation and brand become at risk.

Another example has been occurring on YouTube or Instagram, when celebrities and stars say or post the wrong message and have their accounts deleted, wiping out in an instant all of the brand awareness and recognition they had accrued, including all of the work it took to create that loyal following from millions of users.

The same can happen today, because everything is moving faster and faster, while becoming more and more uncertain. You can learn some key lessons for yourself and your brand. You can't let it stagnate. You always have to grow, innovate, change, evolve, adapt, and pivot.

In the same way, you have to think of your brand as an extension of yourself, your reach, and your influence. What does your following think of you, when your brand comes to mind? This has to do with brand awareness, promotions, marketing, advertising, positioning, and brand leveraging.

If you are dependent upon various social media platforms, then you must abide by their rules and regulations. But, much like building multiple streams of passive income to protect yourself from insurance companies, competitors, job loss, and health issues, you need to build your brand so it becomes independent of any one thing, event, trigger, or platform.

Ways to protect your brand

- ➢ Stay independent. Be dependent upon no one.
- ➢ Multiple streams of income
- ➢ Divide up your products and services so they are not just tied to one name or individual, person or product. That way, if one goes south, the other brands, products, and services are not affected.
- ➢ Divide up how you market and promote, your brand
- ➢ Have multiple accounts on social media platforms (YouTube, Instagram, Facebook, Twitter, Snapchat)
- ➢ Have multiple channels
- ➢ Maintain both physical and digital presences so that, if one goes down, you still have the other.
- ➢ Instead of having one point of failure, engineer multiple areas, thereby stratifying and diversifying potential risks to your brand

across different categories and across time and space.

➢ Divide up your time so you are not tied to your time. If one aspect of your brand is under attack, you can be in different locations, managing it or developing another avenue.

➢ Have an extensive network of individuals and information.

Ways of enhancing your brand

➢ Paid marketing, advertising—both in print and online, including social media

➢ SEO

➢ Free content on your channels (YouTube, Instagram, Facebook, LinkedIn, Snapchat, Twitter)

➢ Word of mouth

➢ Referrals

➢ Followers

➢ Speaking engagements

➢ Books

➢ Digital products

Speaking engagements and books are great, fun ways of enhancing your visibility, promoting yourself, getting the word out, and building, leveraging, and strengthening your brand.

These extensions spread your message, like extra hands and tentacles. The more you expand both horizontally and vertically, the better off you'll be. Think of Amazon or Walmart.

After you get brand awareness and start gaining traction, then you have to figure out ways of automating your business. Amazon invested heavily in logistics and automation; now they are set to dwarf their competitors (and most worldwide economies).

CHAPTER 6

CLIENTS

THIS CHAPTER WILL LOOK at a consultant's clients. This includes:

- ➢ Landing your first few clients
- ➢ Fee setting, billing, and collection
- ➢ Setting the scope and goals of an assignment
- ➢ Contracts
- ➢ Managing client expectations, client retention and satisfaction, and repeat business
- ➢ Negotiating your consulting fees
- ➢ Marketing and business development

> ➢ Tips for physically surviving long assignments

Landing your first few clients

Starting your own business is hard work. It takes a lot of guts and courage to transition from employee into the self-employed and the business owner categories. In the beginning, fear and inertia are the emotions that can hold you back. Your self-doubt, fears, and the comments and criticisms by others can set you back, if you allow them.

But in this phase, you have to plow forward. This is the part of building a consulting business where most people look and say it's too hard, and then quit and turn back.

The most famous people started from nothing and built from there. During my first years as a consultant, I had no clients and was still working residency-level hours. But I was building my knowledge, education, experience, and skillset. Then, one day, I landed my first client, my first sale. It wasn't much, but it led me to build my side hustle into being a full-time income. There are numerous stories of writers, artists, photographers, producers, musicians, and speakers who have started from this paradigm, some well-known and some who are not.

So, you have to keep at it. It is a numbers game. But the more doors you knock on, the greater the probability you'll close your first client. You have to develop faith and trust in the process.

Your first few clients can be associates or colleagues; maybe picked up through word of mouth. They can range from people who found you on the Internet to someone who noticed your promotion on major websites. (Remember the chapter on promotion, marketing, social media, and branding. The more you put yourself out there, promote, market, and brand, the more likely you'll be successful.)

Eventually, you will attract a following and, if you do things correctly, create raving fans.

If you follow these concepts, steps, and suggestions to focus on creating rather than competing, then, instead of being a small fish in a big pond, you will be the only fish or you'll be the biggest fish in a small pond. You want to be the only, best you, and not a different version of someone or something else.

Keeping clients

Not only do you want to land sales, you want to keep clients.

As you grow and expand your business, your client base will come from existing clients as well as new or existing leads. It takes more time to generate new leads, follow up with those leads, and sell new clients than it does to keep an existing client.

Additionally, your business should grow through positive word of mouth, reviews, and references, as well as your social media base and followers. As long as you keep executing, keep delivering exceptional value, under-promise, and over-deliver, your clientele should continue to grow, very much like any clinical practice.

Setting scope and goals of the assignment

Meet with the client face to face, and iron out scope of work, expectations, and goals. Always leave the meeting with a written agreement.

It should include an exact payment structure, the total fee, due dates for project assignments, and payment due dates, as well. Be sure it specifies:

- ✓ Goal and objective
- ✓ Due dates
- ✓ Reporting requirements
- ✓ Where the services are to be performed
- ✓ Required resources
- ✓ Defined expectations and outcome
- ✓ Includes methods for measuring success
- ✓ Provisions for additional fees, if additional work is required

You want to avoid scope creep, which is when the client's requirements and expectations increase as the project proceeds. You end up doing more work for the same pay, in these situations, so you want to avoid this.

Also avoid flat fees. Fees should be set for a scope of work, as well as your time involvement. Any additional requests and any additional time involvement should be negotiated with the client, to reconfirm the project scope and fees.

How to negotiate and how to say no

Consulting is a game of negotiating. Give and take. Learn how to say no. If it is a difficult client or one with a bad reputation, it is easier to avoid getting into the situation in the first place than it is to dig yourself out, regardless of how much they are paying you.

Contracts

Have everything spelled out in writing. Then, with your client, go over it, word for word. Where possible, have an attorney either physically present or on your staff.

Managing client expectations

Establish realistic client expectations and goals early on, through written contracts and constant, clear communication.

This is the most important part, because, without clients, you have no business. Consulting is ultimately a business about people.

Always under-promise and over-deliver. The most important aspects are your client relationships, delivering exceptional customer service, maintaining open and honest communication, creating clear boundaries, and clear, positive intentions for you and the client, without letting your clients walk all over you.

Once you learn how to effectively manage client expectations, deliver an outstanding product or service, under-promise and over-deliver, plus establish open and honest communication, you will be able to work with the best intentions in mind.

CHAPTER 7

NUTS AND BOLTS OF RUNNING YOUR CONULTING BUSINESS

Negotiating your consulting fee

As mentioned previously, effective negotiating is a skillset that can be developed. Undercharge and you not only do a disservice to yourself, but you tell clients you are "worth" less than what you deserve. A higher price point attracts higher quality clients.

Do not be afraid to charge what you think you're worth. It will be hard at first, but remember that once you have established yourself as a credible expert and proven that you can deliver outstanding quality, on time, and at an affordable price, then your market value increases, and you can charge more. When I first started, I would pitch my rate, and I can remember speaking about my experience, qualifications, and successes without any difficulty or hesitation. But I could feel my chest and throat tighten up and butterflies in my stomach when the client asked my consulting fee. Now I know, if the client takes the first offer, then I could have charged more and have left money on the table.

The highest paid consultants make in excess of five hundred to thousands of dollars per hour. Some of the most successful entrepreneurs, business titans, and investors—Oprah, Tony Robbins, Michelle Obama, Jeff Bezos—can value their time at tens of thousands or even hundreds of thousands of dollars per minute. That's how lucrative this field can be, depending upon the value you bring to the table.

Fee setting and bill collection

This is an important section in the book, because it deals with how you get paid in the form of money for your time, services, products, and experience.

The amount you can make is unlimited and depends upon the value you create for the marketplace. Consultants can make anywhere from $100 an hour, starting out, to $1,000 an hour or more, depending upon their time, experience, services, and value.

Your rate is also commensurate with how effective you are at marketing, advertising, and using social media and video to build a following. It correlates to your skills at building teams, being a manager and a leader, and how prolific you are in terms of productivity (publishing books and other content, arranging to hold seminars and do speaking engagements, attracting clients, and building repeat customers).

Initially, your income will be variable and your client base will be sparse. However, over time, you will certainly accumulate more and more of both. In addition, you will discover different ways of scaling your time.

For example, if you're delivering a seminar (either online or in person), the more paying clients you have in the room, the greater your per-hour rate will be, because, after all, the time and space are all there. The more people you can sell into your programs and at the seminar, the more value you'll be able to create, which will in turn lead to more profits.

In terms of billing, collection, and payments, it is important to have an electronic bill recording, selection, and payments program.

I personally use PayPal, Square, and Venmo, to offer more selection to my customers. However, I recommend you select only a single software program to keep track of all of your billing and expenses. Quicken is great, for example, to keep track of all your billings and expenses in one location. Automate all of your payments, billings, invoices, and statements, so you're ready when you file your quarterly IRS tax returns.

Another tip is to require new clients pay an upfront deposit, with the remainder of your invoice to be paid at the end of the assignment, so no one is screwed out of any money. This upfront deposit protects you, in case the client doesn't pay later. And having the balance be due and payable at the end protects your client, in the event of non-completion of the assignment.

Marketing and business development

The key goal of your marketing and business development efforts is to get repeat business and repeat clientele.

My top strategies are:

* Build relationships based on trust
* Exceed relationships
* Get word of mouth, reviews, and references

* Networking. Socializing. Always giving something of value. Being cooperative.
* Go to as many seminars and conferences as possible. Reach out to as many people who can help you or with whom you can develop a positive relationship around your niche.
* Writing your own books on areas of your expertise
* Writing for others
* Getting your articles published
* Doing presentations and lectures
* Keeping in contact

Some of the following action steps have led me to great assignments, including:

* Posting frequently on social media sites like LinkedIn, Facebook, Instagram
* Doing a fantastic job so that word of mouth spreads and you get great reviews
* Writing—you get to be creative, plus you are producing something and getting credit for

it. It is free and only costs you time. Good things come to those who write. It leads to more assignments and opportunities—to write again, speak, do lectures, coach, and do consulting projects. Publishing articles and books on your expertise also helps develop your leadership niche.

* Public speaking—begin with guest lectures and participate in others' seminars. Start by speaking on other people's stages, either paid or for free. Use these events to promote your own products and services. Speaking opportunities also help brand you as a leader in your field. Eventually, you can scale and grow this business, leading to your own seminars.

When people are first starting out, I get the question a lot about the concept of the connection between time and money. They are both finite resources, but you can always make, create, get, and save more money. However, you can never get back time or make more time, except to save more. So, do you have excess of both? Or just one?

Oftentimes, I would fret about each and every expense, so I made a rule for myself: if I could save, make, or get something of equal or greater in value, then I would let go of the worry. Building any business involves the interplay between these two fundamental factors. If you have both, that's great. You are in great position.

If, however, you are like most solo startups, you will invariably have to trade one or the other or both, to achieve your desired results and outcomes. Most businesses put in a lot of time, energy, and sweat equity in the beginning, in order to build that momentum and traction, and they save money on the immediate horizon for future prosperity.

However, some startups have capital that will allow them to bypass a lot of the initial sweat equity that needs to be built up in order to get the business going. So, saving money in and of itself can be a good thing, but if it costs you more time in the long run, it's up to you to determine if that time is wasted by

saving money, or if you're better off spending that
money to save yourself time.

CHAPTER 8

TIPS FOR SURVIVING A LONG-TERM CONSULTING ASSIGNMENT

INVEST IN COMFORT. I came upon this idea late in my career. Earlier on, I was all about saving money, bootstrapping, keeping costs low, going for maximal profit, and analyzing every expense and purchase to see if it was worth it or not or if I could find another non-monetary means of achieving the same result or outcome.

Then, after two years of non-stop traveling through airports, sleeping in airports and different hotels, eating at different restaurants, and never going home, the fast-paced lifestyle began to wear on me. The finances were awesome, but the energy and personal toll my career was taking on me began to take form.

Then, one day, my brother-in-law gave me this idea. We were discussing comfort and style for business travels, and I had this realization: Your energy, piece of mind, and rest are all important to you while on the road. For some long-term, out-of-town assignments, you will be away from family, friends, neighbors, and coworkers, sleeping in places temporarily, so prioritize making arrangement for whatever makes you more comfortable.

So, for example, taking a taxi versus taking an Uber/Lyft versus getting a ride versus public transportation. Since I am frugal by nature, if public transportation takes a bit longer but it's not a big hassle and results in significant cost savings, I will take public transportation and use that extra time toward productivity (audiobooks, business calls, thinking, planning, strategizing, and executing), while on the way. To other people, saving that extra time may be more important to them, and they may elect to pay more. Again, we come to the idea of the which is mightier, the pen or the sword? Are you strapped for time or strapped for capital? Through this prism, you can weigh the pros and cons of each transportation option.

Then apply the same strategy to selecting the following, all through the prism of ensuring your comfort and the quality of your travel/consulting experience:

- ✓ First class versus economy class.
- ✓ Check-in luggage versus carry-on.
- ✓ Lounges versus waiting areas.
- ✓ Hotel brand. Here I recommend you invest in a fantastic hotel brand. Personally, I always stay in Marriott hotels. I have their Marriott Bonvoy credit card, too, so I get credit and points for each stay.

   I pick a hotel chain within the brand that has a nice, safe, and comfortable location near my assignment. I look for one that has free coffee, water, amenities, free continental breakfast, snacks, and happy hours. Also, one that has a 24/7 workout facility, good security, and a fast, reliable Internet connection.

✓ Airlines. I use Google Flights to book my travel. It gives the lowest airfares by date, departure city, and departure times. They also have price alerts so that you know any price discounts. I have used this service to score tons of savings on flights.

✓ Rental cars. I personally use Avis, Hertz, or National. Like hotels, I recommend you pick one company and stick with it. That way, for each project, you get the maximum points that accumulate to rewards over time.

While away, like at home, stick to a routine. I recommend going to bed early. Invariably, most assignments require you to be up and out by 5 a.m. and back in the later parts of the day. On most assignments, I had a personal regimen where I would come back from the project site, go for a one-hour run, eat, and then talk to my wife and family. Then I would wrap up the day.

Set personal and professional goals, and establish daily habits. For example, I read books in business, management, leadership, and finance, as well as cutting-edge books in personal development. Audiobooks are awesome. Don't forget to network and socialize with your fellow colleagues.

Remember to keep and stay hydrated. Eat plenty of fruits and vegetables. Use alcohol to a minimum. Eat healthy. It is easy to get off of this path, but I suggest you force yourself to invest in your own health. I gained ten pounds on one project and had to work really hard to work it off. This will go miles in terms of your energy, mood, outlook, and productivity.

It sounds funny, but think of yourself as an athlete. Not only do you need rest, food, hydration, but you also need to invest in comfort and things that have intangible benefits that can save you time, hassle, worry, and frustration, and that can eliminate energy drains from you. These will all be well worth it.

When on the road, look for the local Whole Foods, Central Market, vegan restaurants, Jamba Juice, and the like. There are plenty of options available for us today that are reliable, fresh, and healthy.

Invest in an eye mask, a neck pillow, and a nice set of headphones to use while you are sleeping. This goes without saying, but remember proper hygiene—shaving, laundry, gum, deodorant, cologne, and soap. Consulting is all about appearances and perceptions. You want to project an air of competence, confidence, and professionalism.

Invest in TSA Clear or TSA Pre-Check. Due to increasing regulations and screening times, you don't want to be waiting in line for thirty minutes or more while TSA agents review IDs and boarding passes, ask you to take off your shoes, and scan all your carry-ons.

With TSA Precheck, you can bypass the long regular lines. It is good for five years and costs less than a hundred bucks—well worth it. Still, always carry less than three ounces of liquids, gels, and soaps. Generally, though, do bring a carry-on, and don't check in anything you don't have to. This will save you at least fifteen to twenty minutes at the check-in counter and more at baggage claim.

Invest in technology, like a great iPhone, iPad, and laptop, so you can read articles and ebooks, watch movies or your favorite TV shows, and catch up on work and email anywhere you are. Use FaceTime, Skype, and WhatsApp plus texting to keep in constant communication with family and friends.

Invest in online certification courses. I do this frequently. When I have downtime, I am investing in my education by taking online certification courses from the Harvard Business School Online. This keeps you accountable (paying the price for the course), makes sure you complete it, and ensures full participation. It only takes two hours a day. At the end of it, you have something to show for your time and efforts, and you can put it on your résumé.

In addition to MOOCs through various universities, CoursEra and Udemy have great resources for any field you may be interested in learning about.

Always have your own personal side projects going on. For example, I wrote all of my books in the wee hours of the night and early morning, during my spare time. I was always networking which led me to future consulting assignments.

Points and loyalty points/cards go a long way. I have gotten free tickets, rental days, free hotel nights, upgrades, and bonuses by being a loyal member. It adds up!

Get paid by making purchases. Get a credit card with 0% APR for the first fifteen months, free sign-up bonuses, and 0% international fees. Get paid and rewarded to spend for your business expenses.

When traveling or working abroad, always pay in the country's currency. Partner with a bank that has zero ATM fees, gives great exchange rates, and charges no foreign transaction fees. Credit cards and ATMs are the way to go these days.

It's also very important to know how to manage your energy and cope with dips and changes. I recommend:

> Staying grounded, being authentic, standing in your own truth, and allowing yourself to be you.

> Be your own highest authority; allow yourself to be you, to make mistakes, to be human, and to authentically and unapologetically express your highest self through your highest intentions.

> Being on your path, knowing your purpose. Don't compare yourself to anyone or anybody.

> Focus. Protect your mental energy from people who drag you down and from distractions. Much like time, your energy is just as precious, so invest it where it matters. Isaiah Hankel, in the *Science of Intelligent*

Achievement, recommends that the first two hours of the day be focused on the most important tasks, when mental engagement and focus are the highest. Then delegate low-priority tasks such as telephone calls, emails, and non-urgent in-person appointments to parts of the day when your energy levels are depleted.

➤ Build up your aerobic capacity, to be able to handle the day-to-day activities of everyday life. I find that running four to eight miles per day (with three to five three-minute sprint intervals), five to six days a week, goes a long way in improving your energy.

➤ Stretching.

➤ Meditating.

➤ Taking cold showers.

➤ Getting eight to ten hours of rest each night and plenty of hydration and exercise each day.

➤ Eating lots of vegetables, fruits, nuts, grains, water, berries, and healthy fats, like avocados

- ➢ Avoiding carbohydrates, sugar, oil, hydrogenated fats, and processed foods.
- ➢ Having a plan and strategy for dealing with the negativity of the world and difficult people.
- ➢ Setting boundaries with people and technology. Set up alerts, so there are no unannounced meetings.
- ➢ Socializing.
- ➢ Reading, watching your favorite movies, and TV shows.
- ➢ Spending time outdoors and in nature.
- ➢ Talking with family and friends.

CHAPTER 9

SPOTTING, CREATING & CAPITALIZING ON EMERGING CONSULTING OPPORTUNITIES

THIS IS PERHAPS my favorite part of the book, because the possibilities are endless. I am always thinking of new ways of monetizing ideas, products, services, and trends. It is innate in me. It is built into me. My friends, family, and colleagues say the same thing about me, which I was unaware of. I frequently spend part of my day thinking about the future: where it's going, current trends, and how to capitalize on these emerging trends, either through investments, new products, services, or how to position myself and my company, build new business revenue models, and develop new sources of revenue streams.

I will highlight several examples to illustrate my points. For example, I am interested in technology, because I've witnessed its power since 1994 and the way it has transformed our lives. I believe the next twenty years will be even more influenced by technology.

I am particularly fascinated with technology's ability to destroy and transform industries overnight. And I say this not because I enjoy seeing businesses go by the wayside, but rather because I am fed up with the existing status quo and the lack of people's sense of urgency (or perhaps they don't even care). I also dislike the excessive bureaucratic rules and regulations, the ways the status quo has benefited the few and ignored the rest, and how we have all been brainwashed into group-think and old, outdated, ineffective models of viewing the way the world works. I am disappointed in how America has gone from a country of prosperity to a country of consumerism, materialism, disease, poverty, mediocrity, inequality, racism, gun violence, terrorism, corruption, and bureaucracy, losing out to developing countries throughout Europe and Asia.

So, in order to spot, create, and capitalize on emerging opportunities, you always have to be reading, talking with others, and thinking. You can either find a need and fill it, or you can find a problem and seek a solution. You also need to figure out more ways to help and serve more people. If you figure out how to help and serve a billion people, you are on your way to becoming a multi-millionaire and even a billionaire.

For myself, I am always asking what are the emerging trends, and how can I serve more people.

I am constantly reading, looking at how others design their marketing and advertising campaigns, and studying how they are leveraging social media and technology within their companies and businesses.

I look to include in my reading ideas that are contrary to mainstream. Then I can think about how this will apply in the next twenty to thirty years. For example, the following ideas are going to be obsolete or will see radical change in the next decade:

> Saving money. It makes no sense to do this, when the central banks can keep interest rates at zero, print trillions of dollars to benefit the ultra-rich, invest that money into asset bubbles, and leave the remaining population on the hook in the form of higher taxes after they burst. Plus, by the time you save a million dollars, you will be in your later stages of life, and the effects of inflation will have eroded your purchasing power.

Here's a question for you: How long will it take you to make and save a million dollars by working versus learning how to become a multi-millionaire investor versus learning how to create over a million dollars in value and how to borrow a million dollars for your startup company? Saving money is not ideal in the traditional sense, because you would need a high-paying job that you would spend a lot of hours at and pay a shitload of taxes on, in contrast to a business owner or investor making a million dollars. Completely different game (Note: it is important to spend less than you earn, but it is not wise to "save" money and kill yourself in every sense of the word.)

➢ Working hard versus working smart AND hard. You need to be selective and strategic in your focus, time, attention, and efforts; do not just go around aimlessly working hard.

➢ Using student loans to finance your education. I am a strong proponent of education. I am a huge advocate for education, learning, collaborating, and growing. You can get a great education at some institutions of higher education, and not so much at others. Will it require $50,000+ per year tuition? I highly doubt it.

Education in America has become a business, where institutions of higher education have been able to increase fees, so as to increase revenues. I am not against capitalism. However, the student loan bubble is currently at $1.5 trillion dollars and rising. What will happen when hundreds of thousands of college graduates have no income to pay off their expensive degrees? Colleges use student athletes to promote their sports programs to increase their revenues in terms of sponsorships, endorsements, merchandise, and media broadcasts.

I am not saying, "Do not go to college," nor am I advocating that you drop out of college. Nine times out of ten, if you do that, you will be worse off than if you had just stayed. Additionally, there are many intangible benefits that college offers including: self-discovery, making your professional contacts, and your social network of friends and relationships. However, the value of an undergraduate education has been commoditized such that someone with a degree from a public university has the ability to do better than someone from a private university.

I had this realization firsthand. I went to public university on a full-tuition scholarship, did well, graduated with no student loan debt, and got into my first choice of a top-tier medical school. Some of my classmates who went to the Ivy Leagues after high school didn't do as well there and had to settle on lesser medical schools, while some couldn't even get in. That, in my opinion, is a waste of money: to pay so much to go to an Ivy League school, yet having your options limited. I thought getting an Ivy League education was supposed to give you an advantage in your career and in life!

So, you should factor in the cost of an education, where you want it to take you, and also have a plan and strategy in place to have the degree pay off, rather than just attend a school based on its prestige or name brand.

Again, just getting a high-cost Ivy or selective school education just for the sake of getting the degree is group-think and outdated, ineffective advice. There has to be an objective reason or purpose for investing that amount of money towards higher education.

What a good pedigree does give you, though, is credibility. If you have a legitimate advanced degree (MD, PhD, JD, MBA) from a reputable institution, what it does is brand you as being competent and trustworthy, so clients are more likely to buy from you and trust you, compared to someone who has no such qualifications.

I also noticed this personally. Even though I hated working in the medical profession, my MD-PhD degree from great institutions gave me huge credibility to market and sell my products, services, and experiences to my clients.

Again, you have to weigh the pros and cons of pursuing these advanced degrees in terms of cost, time, and energy versus the opportunity costs. Individuals such as Mark Zuckerberg, Steve Jobs, and Bill Gates (all college dropouts) are few and far between. Don't think that just because you drop out of school it means you're on your way toward becoming the next tech billionaire! I don't recommend that.

➢ Getting a high-paying job instead of creating assets that pay you more in less time with less taxes and with more leverage. Getting a high-paying job means you will be working hard for money, the government, and the banks. However, if you generate the same amount of income from investments or businesses, you will be working to create assets, which will result in increased passive income and higher gains in less time, with less effort, as well as significant tax deductions.

➢ Planning to work for the same company for thirty-plus years. Old school idea.

➢ Climbing the corporate ladder. Old school idea.

➢ Retiring when you turn sixty-five. Old school idea. People are retiring in their twenties, thirties, and forties already.

➢ Buying a million-dollar house. Old school idea.

➢ Buying a fancy car means that you're wealthy. This is known as the thirty-thousand dollar "millionaire."

➢ Investing in the American Dream. This is gone.

➢ Thinking that pensions and Social Security are going to provide the majority of your income in the future. Dangerous, Old School idea.

➢ Getting married. This is starting to make no sense to me. This is a societal-based construct. Most people spend over $50,000 on a wedding! That just doesn't make any sense. With the current divorce rate over sixty percent, this makes even less sense: Why would you spend a huge amount of time and money on the relationship, pay for an expensive wedding, and then have half of your assets wiped out in divorce, knowing full well the odds of that happening are over sixty percent of the time, and do it multiple times throughout your life? Now I know why Hollywood celebrities and stars approach marriage from a completely different perspective.

Prior to the Trump Administration, I was paying more taxes as a result of being married than had I still been single, even when making the same amount of income. In other words, from a financial standpoint, you were "penalized" for getting married.

Many millennials now have partners or elect to stay single. They still pursue relationships, but many do not "get married," in the traditional sense. I believe this idea of getting married is or will fall by the wayside in coming generations when you take into account the financial aspects.

➤ Having kids. Don't get me wrong. I love my nephew, Kai, and my nieces (Tiffany, Tina, Sophia, Aubrey, Olivia, and Sabrina). You have to ask yourself if having a kid fits into your life plan. Kids are a significant investment in emotion, time, energy, and finances.

That means not just having kids because that is "the thing to do." I made this same mistake, following group-think, when I pursued a medical career.

I think I would have a nervous breakdown if I had kids, because I would constantly worry about whether they were being properly fed, sheltered, and kept safe. Plus, with terrorism, racism, gun violence, crimes, and bullying so much part of our current culture, and the stresses on parents to make sure children get a good education, find the right partner, discover their life purpose, and are able to pursue their passions, find prosperity, success, and happiness, along with it being harder and harder to eke out an existence, we have decided that having a kid is not in my wife's and my immediate future.

The ideas above are all mainstream BS, fed and fueled by political campaigns, media advertising, big corporations, and special interests.

Here are some personal examples where I have benefited from spotting trends and capitalizing on opportunities:

* Being an early investor in Bitcoin back in 2010. Reading about this new technology, I had a "hunch" it was going to be something big.

* Seeing that Airbnb had a huge potential and how being a host and traveler depended upon reviews and ratings. So, I started building up my Airbnb profile (much like with eBay).

✶ And countless other investing opportunities in real estate and stocks.

These have all come about based on my spotting, creating, and capitalizing on emerging market opportunities. I believe that, just as the Internet and globalization have taken out blue-collar jobs, automation, artificial intelligence, and virtual-augmented reality will take out white-collar jobs.

The *Wall Street Journal* and *Investor's Business Daily* are both great places to read about current trends, topics, and ideas. They are ideal for getting business ideas, and for spotting, identifying, and capitalizing on emerging opportunities. Also, read the marketing materials developed by your colleagues, co-workers, and competitors.

This is a skillset you can develop. Even more powerful is when you can develop the ability to create trends. Those who do are called trendsetters, which are extremely prevalent in sports, business, media, entertainment, fashion, and the creative fields.

The more you read, think, analyze, talk with others, and educate yourself, the more you will be able to recognize trends and potential new areas of consulting, and the payoff is huge.

CHAPTER 10

UNIQUE CHALLENGES

Pacing Yourself

Starting in 2016, I went full-steam, pursuing, building, and developing my consulting career. I was fed up with the medical profession and intent on succeeding as a consultant. I became a workaholic, transferring my hundred-plus-hour work weeks into my consulting career—constantly networking, studying, reading, learning, working out, working, and traveling.

Needless to say, my unhappiness with the medical profession transferred over to my consulting and business career, where I became burned out, stressed out, and unhappy in my personal life. I found myself irritable, angry, and impatient. My workaholism was a symptom of a larger underlying issue.

I realized that I needed to prioritize my work-life balance over just making money or my mental, physical, and emotional health as well as my marriage would suffer. I had the sudden realization that, if I did not change, I would end up dead, hospitalized, institutionalized, in jail, or alone. So, I proactively made changes, and now, my family, personal life, and marriage are the better for it. We still have struggles and issues, but I take a more proactive approach to problem-solving. I am not just working the problem away and thinking that making more money is going to solve everything.

Difficult clients

Avoid them at all costs. They are not worth your time, effort, or energy, despite what they may pay.

Non-paying clients or late-paying clients

Again, do not deal with these types of individuals. Fire them on the spot. You will waste so much time and effort that could be directed toward better paying, easier to deal with clients, and better opportunities.

Low-balling clients

This goes back to character and integrity. Those clients who try to low-ball you do it more out of a character issue. These individuals are also more likely to pay late, not pay at all, or come up with unjustified reasons not to pay you for your work.

For new clients

Do small, low-investment, low-risk projects that involve only a small time commitment. See how it is to work with them. See if they pay on time. If they don't, do not waste your time. Fire them on the spot. In this day and age, there is no shortage of good clients. Do not get yourself into situations where clients can cheat, steal, or rip you off. And there are plenty of review sites—use them!

Haters

As you gain success, you will invariably "attract" haters. This was extremely prevalent in the medical profession, which is filled with a scarcity, hoarding mentality, and a competitive versus cooperative ethos. Many people were in the field for pure ego-centric reasons. I should know, because I was one of them.

Haters are people who secretly envy you and want you to fail, either because they themselves have failed or they don't have the balls to "man up" and go for it. Oftentimes, they secretly have a fear of success and/or failure.

This is human nature, and we must learn to recognize it, deal with it, and develop strategies to manage these situations and these types of individuals.

They will do things such as bad mouth you (usually behind your back, because they have no spine to tell you to your face), go onto social media and post fake reviews, or use the threat of an unjustified negative review to try to manipulate you. What a loser mentality, in the sense of where they are coming from.

My suggestion is pay them no attention. This is easier said than done, sure, but do not get involved with these types of individuals. As you keep your ground, stay connected, stay true to yourself, and keep your intentions clear, these haters will fade into the distance.

As you focus more and more on creating value, developing great relationships with open and honest communication, and over-delivering, these haters will fall by the wayside, and you will attract better and more attractive clientele on each project, who are more enjoyable to work with and for. You will also attract a loyal following. Keep executing, keep producing, and keep adding and creating value.

A close mentor of mine said, "Don't mind the chickens. When the chickens come out and peck, an eagle soars higher and higher, until the chickens don't even register on the radar."

I have noticed this firsthand while hiking tall mountains. At the bottom are the masses. As you trek upwards, the view gets better, the air becomes more fresh, and it's no longer crowded. So just keep trekking. This is the "Law of Sowing and Reaping" or the "Law of Karma." What goes around comes around, usually ten- or a hundred-fold. So, keep sowing good seeds, and success will come to you, for sure.

Another close mentor of mine said, "At first, they ignore you. Then they hate on you. Then they wish they were you." Remember the section in Chapter 3 on your consulting niche.

Think about this: if they have the time to go and try to sabotage your success, you must be doing something right. Because if they're spending their precious time trying to take you down, instead of furthering themselves, it must mean they have an awful lot of time to waste on unproductive, meaningless things and are probably living meaningless lives themselves.

And LeBron James said of his haters once (along these lines). If they have time to sabotage and backstab you, they are probably unsuccessful. Think about it: The people who are successful are on their own paths and not distracted or wasting their time trying to take other people down.

Developing a high-quality product and service

This section goes without saying. You should always aim for delivering an exceptional-quality product and service. Not only to stay in business, but because it's good in practice. It's a matter of integrity. Not doing a good job will not only jeopardize your next gig and maybe put you out of business, but it's the principle that matters.

Always aim to promise low and then deliver more than you promise.

A special note on difficult clients: sometimes, no matter how far you go, some clients will never be satisfied. This is a matter of character. Some clients will try to low-ball you and expect the world from you. This is their reality, coming from a frame of scarcity and exploitation rather than abundance and cooperation.

My advice with these types of clients is to screen them very carefully and avoid doing business with them, as it will not be worth the time and effort. Use that time elsewhere—it's better spent on other clients who are more worthy.

CONCLUSION

IS CONSULTING FOR YOU? A consulting career can be highly lucrative, rewarding, and professionally fulfilling. But your future is in your hands.

In this book, I have outlined the path toward a consulting career. I have laid out the steps for transitioning from a traditional career into a consulting career. I have outlined the advantages and disadvantages of starting a consulting career, as well as how to develop your niche.

This includes building and developing your brand, brand protection and enhancement, and the skilled use of technology. I showed how to heighten brand awareness and use word of mouth to position and leverage yourself and your brand.

I have described the nuts and bolts of running a successful consulting business and outlined the top five skillsets needed to become a successful consultant.

In the last part of the book, I have outlined the issues around dealing with clients: generating leads, following up on leads, landing the sale, fee setting, bill collection, marketing and business development, as well as provided tips for surviving on the road as a consultant.

Finally, I highlight the unique challenges you will encounter, including developing a high-quality product or service, over-communicating, using open and honest communication, under-promising, and over-delivering, plus establishing clear intentions and setting clear boundaries. I have also described how to deal with new clients, as well as difficult clients and haters.

###

If you're further interested in private client coaching, speaking engagements, or a free fifteen-minute coaching consultation, reach out to me at chL1357@gmail.com.

Again, to your continued success!

ABOUT THE AUTHOR

DR. CHRISTOPHER LOO is a physician who became financially free at the age of twenty-nine and retired early at the age of thirty-eight, as a result of making strategic investments after the 2008 financial crisis. A graduate of the MD-PhD program offered jointly through the Baylor College of Medicine and Department of Bioengineering at Rice University, he is the author of *How I Quit My Lucrative Career and Achieved Financial Freedom*

Using Real Estate and three other Physician's Guides for financial freedom.

He is the host of the *Financial Freedom for Physicians* podcast, a regular contributor to KevinMD, and has spoken about the importance of financial literacy for Passive Income MD, the White Coat Investor, Board Vitals, SEAK Non-Clinical Careers, SoMe Docs, Doximity, Medpage Today, FinCon, and other high-profile financial brands geared toward high-income professionals.

His website is www.drchrisloomdphd.com.

###

Books by Christopher H. Loo

How I Quit My Lucrative Medical Career and Achieved Financial Freedom Using Real Estate (You Can, Too!)

The Physician's Guide to Financial Freedom Using Stocks and Options

The Physician's Guide to Financial Freedom: Getting Started as a Consultant

The Physician's Guide to Financial Freedom: Becoming a Freelance Writer